Strategic Planning for Catholic Parishes

Listening, Learning, and Responding through the lens of Pope Francis's teachings on synodality

Strategic Planning for Catholic Parishes: Listening, Learning, and Responding through the lens of Pope Francis's teachings on synodality

ISBN: 978-1-950721-16-0

Editing and design by Harshman Services

Published by Harshman House Publishing

PO Box 82

Spring Valley, IL 61362

Author's Note:

Why I Wrote This Book

My goal in writing this book is to help parishes discern God's calling for their leadership and parishioners. I hope to see reinvigorated parishes that are committed to listening, learning and continuous improvement. In my work with Catholic parishes, I often find people recognize the value of long-term planning but don't know where to start. Some of these parishes are in survival mode and struggle to find the necessary time to plan for a vibrant future. In addition, many Catholic parishes aren't able to pay an outside consultant to lead strategic planning. This book provides parishes with a flexible framework for an inclusive planning process that is rooted in the spirit of synodality as described by Pope Francis. It is time for parishes to develop and articulate a bold vision for the future. The book has been written for pastors, parish staff members, parish councils, and other lay leaders.

Consultants who are looking for specific advice on working with Catholic parishes will also benefit from this book. I've included sample templates, letters, surveys, prayers, and agendas to help parish leaders facilitate a successful strategic planning process.

Download blank templates and samples for free!

As a thank you for buying this book, you can access templates and samples for free.

To download, go to: *catholic.tadickel.com*

Contents

Section 1

An Introduction to Synodality and Strategic Planning

Chapter 1

Setting the Stage

"Master, we have worked hard all night and have caught nothing,
but at your command I will lower the nets."

When I think about Catholic parish strategic planning, the passage Luke 5:1–11 comes to mind. Simon Peter and some of the other disciples had been fishing all night with nothing to show for their efforts. Jesus had been teaching a crowd on the shore and saw two boats at the water's edge. He got in one boat with Simon Peter, and after teaching the crowds from the lake, he instructed the disciple and his fellow fisherman to take it out to deeper water and lower their nets again. The disciples were tired after a long, unsuccessful night, and reluctant to cast their nets again. But Simon Peter clearly saw something in Jesus and told him, "at your command I will lower the nets."

The gospel passage goes on to say that they caught so many fish that their nets were tearing. While Simon Peter's initial reaction was to claim his own unworthiness, he and several of his fellow disciples decided to leave everything behind and follow Jesus. As parishioners, staff members and leaders of Catholic parishes, it's easy to become discouraged at times about the future of our Church and parishes. We are called to spread the Good News, but there are many things that get in the way. Like the disciples in this passage, we might be tired, feel unworthy, or be reluctant to open ourselves to the Holy Spirit. We might think we lack the financial resources or the expertise to determine how to plan for the future and move our parishes forward. As Catholics, we were never promised an easy path. Instead, we must have the faith to heed God's call like Simon Peter did. While we will experience challenges at times, we need to look for those affirming moments when the parish community comes together in beautiful worship, support for the grieving, counseling for the afflicted, and outreach for those less fortunate.

"Organizations that want to survive, prosper, and do good and important work must respond to the challenges the world presents. Their response may be to do what they have always done, only better, but they may also need to shift their focus and strategies."[1] This book provides a framework for Catholic parishes to plan for the future. Parishes might consider strategic planning for the following reasons:

1. There is a desire to create a vision for the future.
2. A new pastor is seeking input to chart the course ahead.
3. The parish has experienced changes, growth or a decline in membership and needs to forge a new path forward
4. Parishioners have ideas for the future, and there is a need to formally build consensus around a plan.
5. The parish is in a rut and wants to make changes for the betterment of the church.

After decades of declining mass attendance, membership and vocations, now is the time to embrace change and plan for the future of Catholic parishes. We can do this while staying true to the teachings of the Church. The world is changing faster than ever before, and technology and connectivity are accelerating that transformation. This presents challenges and opportunities alike for parishes to enhance their evangelization efforts. It is comfortable to do what we've always done. But we need to prayerfully consider whether God is calling us to make changes instead.

When the Timing Is not Right for Strategic Planning

There's never a perfect time for strategic planning, but there are instances when this process is not recommended:

1. **Crisis:** Because strategic planning should be a comprehensive, creative, and visionary process, it should not result from a need to address an immediate crisis. Strategic planning during a crisis typically leads to short-term, reactive thinking.

2. **Upcoming change in leadership:** Pastors are ultimately responsible for oversight of a parish. As a result, they must approve strategic plans and set priorities. For this reason, strategic planning is not recommended immediately before a leadership change.

3. **Lack of commitment:** The pastor, staff, and lay leadership need to understand the importance of strategic planning and work together to plan for the future and enact change. If a pastor is not supportive of the effort, the process will likely be a disappointment for those involved.

Chapter 2

What Is Synodality?

Pope Francis has discussed the concept of "synodality" during his papacy, and his decision to convene a three-year process titled "For a Synodal Church: Communion, Participation, and Mission," which will culminate in September 2023, with a Synod of Bishops signals the importance of synodality for the Church. In October 2015, he stated, "The journey of synodality is the journey that God wants from his church in the third millennium. A synodal church is a listening church, aware that listening is more than hearing. It is a reciprocal listening, in which each one has something to learn."[2]

In his speech at the fiftieth anniversary of the institution of the Synod of Bishops in 2015, Pope Francis stated, "What the Lord is asking of us is already in some sense present in the very word *synod*. Journeying together—laity, pastors, the Bishop of Rome—is an easy concept to put into words, but not so easy to put into practice."[3]

A synod is an advisory body of the Catholic Church. It generally refers to the Synod of Bishops, which meets to provide input on matters pertaining to the Church. Diocesan synods can be invoked by bishops to discuss matters applicable to their dioceses.

The three-year synod will be the first "decentralized" process for the universal Church,[4] which means there will be active participation from local dioceses. The synod will have three phases:

- **Diocesan phase:** Consultation and participation of the People of God. This phase will include opportunities for listening, and notes will be sent from dioceses to their episcopal conferences to synthesize into a single report

- **Continental phase:** Dialogue and discernment. Each continental group will create a single report to send to the Vatican's General Secretariat.
- **Universal phase**: The bishops of the world in Rome. The bishops will meet to provide consultation to Pope Francis.

The Vademecum (2021) is a handbook to help guide the local Church in this synodal process. It provides the following guidance:

> The Synodal Process is first and foremost a spiritual process. It is not a mechanical data-gathering exercise or a series of meetings and debates. Synodal listening is oriented towards discernment. It requires us to learn and exercise the art of personal and communal discernment. We listen to each other, to our faith tradition, and to the signs of the times in order to discern what God is saying to all of us.

The Preparatory Document for the synod (2021) describes these fundamental questions to guide the consultation:

> "A synodal Church, in announcing the Gospel, "journeys together." How is this "journeying together" happening today in your particular Church? What steps does the Spirit invite us to take in order to grow in our "journeying together"?

In 2017, The Diocese of Burlington (Vermont) announced a synod to develop a pastoral plan. "I will seek input from all. I will listen to all. I will discern with you all," Bishop Christopher Coyne told Catholics in a post on the diocese's site.[5]

The Diocese of San Diego's Young Adult Synod in 2019 was "a time for young adults to dream big and make decisions about walking with Christ and to engage the local Church to accompany them in the mission of Jesus." That involved listening to adults aged 18 to 39 who were active in the Church, as well as those who considered themselves unaffiliated. As was detailed on that diocese's site, each parish priest chose one young adult to serve as a delegate, along with three others for a total of 240, to participate in the synod. The average age of those who participated in the synod was 26 years.[6]

The Synod for the Amazon opened in 2019 to discuss issues related to the region. According to Hansen, "While other special synods have addressed particular geographical regions like Africa, Asia, and Europe, this is the first one organized around a distinct ecological territory." Leading up to the three-week synod, Pan-Amazonian Ecclesial Network, or Repam, gathered input to inform the synod over a period of two years:

> "Repam coordinated and conducted about 300 listening sessions throughout the region, involving all nine countries in the Amazon. About 22,000 people were directly involved in the territorial assemblies and smaller dialogue groups, and another 65,000 people participated in parish groups. In other places, like Washington D.C., Rome and Bogotá, Colombia, various experts joined representatives of Amazon communities to reflect on issues that were being raised in the consultation process."[7]

Many have questioned the meaning of synodality, and Bishop Robert Barron has provided an explanation. "Whatever Pope Francis means by 'synodality,' he quite clearly doesn't mean a process of democratization, or putting doctrine up for a vote. He means, it seems to me, a structured conversation among all of the relevant ecclesial players—bishops, priests, and laity—for the sake of hearing the voice of the Spirit."

Although an inclusive listening process is essential for the path of synodality, more important is an openness and attentiveness to the Holy Spirit. This idea of a "structured conversation . . . for the sake of hearing the voice of the Spirit"[8] and "journeying together"[9] can be applied to strategic planning at the parish level. Only a bishop can invoke a synod, but we can promote Pope Francis's spirit of a "listening church" through the parish strategic planning process.

The synod processes described throughout this book include multiple shared elements, such as inclusivity, discernment, wide input, a structured effort for listening and learning, and a radical openness to the Holy Spirit. Ultimately, it takes a whole community of faithful followers to discern God's calling for a parish or diocese. That's why we must journey together as we seek His will for the future of our Church.

Chapter 3

What Is Strategic Planning, and Why Is it Important?

Does your parish think and act strategically, or does it continue doing the same things and expect different results? I often hear parishes talk about wanting to increase membership, engage more youth, or provide outreach to the less fortunate, but they rarely have a strategy in place to accomplish these goals.

Bryson defines strategic planning "as a deliberative, disciplined approach to producing fundamental decisions and actions that shape and guide what an organization (or other entity) is, what it does, and why."[10]

The world is changing faster than ever before. Technology has made us more connected and provides us with instant access to information. Today 97% of Americans own a cell phone, up from 62% in 2002, according to the Pew Research Center (2021). Eighty-five percent of Americans now own a smartphone, compared with 35% when Pew conducted its first survey of smartphone ownership in 2011. The question is, how have our parishes adapted to these changes?

Technology use has increased, and parishioners have grown accustomed to virtual meetings and live streaming masses.

Our parishes can embrace change while staying true to the teachings of the Catholic Church.

So why is strategic planning important? Strategic planning provides many benefits for parishes and other organizations:

1. **Establishing a vision:** Strategic planning helps parishes establish a vision for a successful future. Many churches are struggling with attendance, collections, membership, and connecting with youth. Strategic planning can help your parish develop an approach for addressing these challenges. Does your parish have a long-term vision for how it will be successful in the future?

2. **Engaging people:** Strategic planning is a great tool to engage people. Like synodality discussed by Pope Francis, strategic planning should provide multiple opportunities for parishioners and non-parishioners to offer feedback and get involved with the implementation of the plan. How can your strategic planning process engage members and nonmembers?

3. **Communicating priorities:** Strategic planning helps parishes communicate priorities to parishioners and the community at large. Many organizations, including Catholic parishes, struggle with communication. Strategic planning processes should include regular communication about parish priorities and progress toward identified goals. How can your parish improve communication of its strategic priorities?

4. **Enhancing mission:** Strategic planning can help parishes signal a new openness to the Spirit and become more intentional about their mission. All strategic goals should be rooted in the parish's mission. Instead of continuing to do things because "that's the way we have always done it," strategic planning helps us choose what we are called to do and what we may need to stop doing.

Despite all these advantages, some parishes still aren't engaged in strategic planning. I find there are three reasons for this:

1. Parishes are too focused on day-to-day survival. In the book *The 4 Disciplines of Execution: Achieving Your Wildly Important Goals*, the authors describe the "whirlwind" of daily responsibilities that consume all organizations and employees. This whirlwind often prevents organizations from focusing on long-term priorities. Parish staff members are frequently underpaid and overworked. As a result, they struggle to set aside time to plan for the future.

2. Parishes, pastors, and lay leaders may be unfamiliar with how to conduct strategic planning. They are uncomfortable with designing a process or creating a plan format that will work for their parish. In my experience, creating a plan is much easier than implementing it. Strategic plan documents and processes can look very different. Your plan will reflect where you are as a parish and where you are going.

3. Parishes struggle to find the right time to begin a strategic planning process. There is no perfect time to begin a planning process. However, there may be less opportune times such as an upcoming leadership transition, major changes in the parish, crisis, or during a busy liturgical season.

None of this is to say strategic planning of any kind is foolproof. Unfortunately, many parishes have been involved with strategic planning processes that have been less than successful. Why does this happen?

Strategic planning processes can fail if the following occurs:

1. **There's a lack of commitment by the leadership.** In order for strategic planning to be successful, there must be buy-in from parish leadership. That includes the pastor or administrator, staff support, and lay volunteers. Often, it's necessary to have someone champion the project to ensure the process moves forward. The champion can be the pastor

or a staff member, but it is often best for this person to be a lay volunteer with credibility in the parish community.

2. **Goals are unclear.** Ambiguous or imprecise goals are the Achilles heel of many strategic plans. Goals should instead be written in a way that people who were not involved in the development of the plan can understand them and know how to achieve them. Strategic planning best practices include identifying measurable goals and timelines.

3. **No plan exists for implementation or accountability.** Frequently organizations develop plans and think the work will just happen. Processes need to be established to implement the plan, identify who is responsible (staff or volunteers), establish deadlines, and determine how the plan will be regularly reviewed.

4. **Future plans are based entirely on past experiences.** It is common for clergy and laity to rely on their past experiences to determine the content of their strategic plan. Incremental change can be effective, but we also need to be bold in our thinking. The world has progressed, and we need to recognize that what we have done before may not be successful in the future. Our past experiences may be limiting in terms of how we relate to what nonpracticing Catholics and non-Catholics are looking for in a parish.

5. **Parishes try to do too much.** Strategic plans can grow beyond what is realistic to accomplish. Parishes benefit more from trying to do a small number of things really well versus being overburdened by unrealistic goals.

How does synodality apply to strategic planning?

As I shared in the previous chapter, strategic planning helps promote Pope Francis's spirit of a "listening church" by engaging the parish and greater community. Strategic planning is a formal process that will help create a greater understanding of a parish's needs and provide a roadmap for how it can prosper in the future. The process in this book is more than just a business model that can be applied to parishes. Rather, it requires us to discard our self-interests and revolutionize our parishes through our openness to the Holy Spirit.

Section 2

Readiness for Strategic Planning and Purpose

Chapter 4

Your Parish Is Ready

Congratulations! If you have read this far into the book, your parish has bought into strategic planning, and you're beginning to think about the future. Now the questions include what's reasonable to expect, and how long will this take?

The following strategic planning timeline is a realistic template for the process. Parishes can accelerate the timeline based on their needs and the availability of core planning team members. In general, parish strategic planning can take anywhere from three to six months.

A six month timeline might look like the following, but it is often condensed to a shorter time period.

July
- Initial meetings
- Selecting the core planning team
- Designing the process
- Reaching conceptual agreement with the process and timeline

August
- Communicating the process to parishioners and the community
- Data collection
- Listening phase: survey and listening sessions

September
- Core planning team retreat

October
- Task forces meet

November
- Task forces meet
- Plan development

December
- Core planning team finalizing the plan
- Focus area teams forming to implement the plan
- Communicating the plan to the parish

January
- Implementation of the strategic plan

This chapter provides an overview of how your parish may begin getting buy-in and designing what the process looks like. A planning and implementation checklist can be found in Appendix A. The checklist is intended to be a guide. However, strategic planning is never a completely linear process, so this should be viewed as a general, flexible framework. The document can be shared with the planning team to keep everyone on the same page.

Getting Buy-In

In order for a parish to succeed with strategic planning, there needs to be buy-in from leadership. It must be accepted that this is an important initiative worthy of the resources required and time necessary for meetings, gathering data, listening to the community, communicating to parishioners, gaining staff support, and developing and implementing the plan. The pastor or administrator of the parish needs to be committed.

In addition, involvement of lay leadership will be important for providing input and helping create and implement the plan. Lay leadership typically includes the parish council and finance council at a minimum. It will also be important to ensure that the staff understands the need for strategic planning.

Designing a Process

Catholic parishes are diverse. Although they share the same faith tradition, they differ in their sizes, demographics, settings, cultures, histories, and customs. It is important to realize that strategic plans and the process required to develop them differ accordingly. However, there are some key components that should be included in all strategic planning processes:

Core Planning Team: Role and Number of People

One of the most important aspects of a successful strategic planning process is assembling the right team to guide this effort. The pastor has the ultimate authority, but he needs a dedicated team of lay people who will advise him throughout the process. I recommend parishes identify a core planning team with about eight members. This ensures the group will be a manageable size while still bringing together diverse perspectives.

Team members should meet the following criteria:

1. **Big-picture thinkers:** Strategic planning requires everyone involved to identify and select major opportunities, issues, and challenges that will impact a parish's future. Team members who understand the big picture and can move away from the minutiae of daily parish life will

provide more valuable insights than those who focus on inconsequential matters.

2. **Open to diverse perspectives:** The team should include diverse perspectives. An inclusive team will have people from various occupations, of different ages and genders, of multiple ethnic and racial backgrounds, some who are newer to the parish, and others who have been there for a long time, for example. Also, as we apply synodality to strategic planning, an important aspect of this process is the ability to listen and learn from people. Team members need to recognize that their perspectives may not represent the parish as a whole. Some prospective core team members may have difficulty empathizing with inactive members or non-Catholics, but it is important to consider various viewpoints.

3. **Free from personal agendas:** Core team members need to set aside their personal agendas and interests to ensure their ideas best serve the parish as a whole.

4. **Credible:** Many people in the parish might be skeptical of the planning process and resulting changes. That's all the more reason to find trusted, credible individuals who have the best intentions of the parish in mind. This credibility will help parishioners understand the importance of strategic planning, encourage them to provide input, and support the implementation of the plan.

5. **Prayerful:** A strategic planning process that's rooted in synodality requires prayerful people who are moved by the Holy Spirit and willing to listen to God's call.

As referenced in the previous chapter, a champion is typically needed to ensure the process goes smoothly. This should be a person who has some proven leadership ability and credibility in the parish. The pastor must respect and trust this person to have the best interests of the parish in mind. Responsibilities may include convening and running meetings.

For some parishes, the core planning team might be the parish council or a subcommittee of the parish council. Other parishes might identify a small number of parishioners. Although it is helpful to have core planning team members with strategic planning experience, that should not be a prerequisite. I recommend having at least a member or two with some strategic planning experience that may have come through nonprofit board service or their work experience.

One question I often receive is whether staff should serve on the core planning team. That depends on the dynamics of the parish and staff. Strategic planning can feel threatening to staff. They may fear their jobs could disappear or change based on the results of the plan. The pastor needs to play a key role. The staff is going to be responsible for implementation, so it is important to think about how they will be involved. They may not need to serve on the core planning team, but they should definitely have opportunities to provide input. It can be valuable to have a staff member serve as a support person for the core planning team, such as helping with meeting notes, scheduling, and communicating with the parish.

The core planning team will need to meet on a regular basis over the course of several months to design the planning process, create the plan, and develop a system for implementing the plan.

Conceptual Agreement

When you decide to embark on a strategic planning process, it's important to develop a conceptual agreement among the core planning team to describe what that process will look like. You'll need to commit to reviewing existing ministries and programs and being open regarding how the parish moves forward. The planning process can take anywhere from three to six months to complete. If it takes too long, you'll lose momentum. If the period is too short, you may not be able to engage enough people or develop a plan that's sufficiently detailed.

I have found that parishes often prefer to kick off strategic planning processes in the fall with the intention of completing the plan by the end of the year and beginning implementation in January. This timeline often coincides with installing new parish council members, and strategic planning happens before the busyness of Thanksgiving, Advent, and Christmas. Alternatively, a strategic planning process might also be launched in January with implementation beginning in the summer.

The core planning team should identify who will be involved with the planning process. Strategic planning is a fantastic opportunity for engagement. I recommend erring on the side of involving too many people. Many parishes have opportunities for input through in-person or virtual listening sessions, surveys, town hall-style meetings, and sharing plan drafts with the parish.

Using an External Consultant

As a strategic planning consultant, I am often asked whether a consultant is necessary to help lead the process. I think it depends. I see some organizations successfully navigate strategic planning processes without a consultant. These organizations typically have staff or volunteers who are skilled and experienced in strategic planning. In addition, a leader of the planning process must have the time necessary to keep things moving along. On the other hand, some organizations choose to use a strategic planning consultant and are happy with the outcome.

This book has been written to empower and enable parishes to lead strategic planning without an external consultant if desired. Your core planning team needs to discuss whether you have the capacity to lead the process on your own. You may also decide to use an external consultant to help with portions of the process such as facilitating listening sessions, administering surveys, or leading meetings during the plan's development phase. This hybrid approach can be helpful and cost effective.

Communicating the Process to the Parish

When initiating a strategic planning process, it's important to communicate to parishioners and other stakeholders what you're doing. Strategic planning should be approached as an exciting opportunity to assess the parish's current state, listen to one another, learn from the parish community, and become more attentive to the Holy Spirit.

Parishioners should know why the process is being initiated and ways they may be able to get involved. For example, they may be invited to complete a survey, attend a listening session, or help with the implementation of the plan.

Appendix B includes a sample letter to the parish introducing the strategic planning process. Parishes can use all mediums to communicate the upcoming process, including traditional mail, email, the bulletin, the parish's website, social media and text message systems. Creating awareness is key.

Chapter 5

What Is Your Purpose?

At the beginning of a strategic planning process, it is important to spend some time discussing the parish's purpose. Each parish has its own unique characteristics and areas of focus that should be articulated in any vision or mission statement.

If your parish already has a vision, mission statement, or both, your core planning team should review and determine whether these statements accurately describe your parish and your vision for the future.

This may be a quick process if your purpose is already clear. If it's not, however, or there's a reason for changing your mission statement or vision, it may take longer.

Some churches only have a mission statement and no vision statement, and that's OK. It can be beneficial for core planning teams to spend some time reviewing other parishes' vision and mission statements. Consider how these statements accurately reflect what God is calling your parish to be.

What Should a Vision and Mission Statement Capture?

A vision statement is focused on the future. It should represent what the parish wants to be. The vision statement is never fully attained and can provide a goal to aspire toward. The vision statement should be concise and memorable.

A mission statement describes what the parish does today to work toward its vision. The mission statement should be succinct and summarize how it accomplishes objectives.

Core Ideology

Besides vision and mission statements, another way to capture your parish's purpose is through core ideology as described by Collins and Porras. They define core ideology as "the enduring character of an organization." They say a core ideology has two parts:

1. "Core values are the essential and enduring tenets of an organization. A small set of guiding principles, core values require no external justification; they have intrinsic value and importance to those inside the organization." Core values for a parish depend on the personality, character, or charism of the parish. Here are a few examples:

   a. Hospitality
   b. Outreach to the poor
   c. Participatory worship
   d. Evangelization
   e. Lay involvement

2. "Core purpose . . . is the organization's reason for being. An effective purpose reflects people's idealistic motivations for doing the company's work . . . it captures the soul of the organization." The core purpose might be synonymous with what some parishes refer to as a vision or mission statement.[11]

Your core planning team can decide whether the more conventional vision or mission statements or core ideology are better descriptors for your parish.

Reviewing Vision and Mission Statements

For each parish, this process is different. Sometimes it's fast ... other times, not so much.

- **The quick review**: I have worked with parishes that review their vision and/or mission statements, and they are in agreement that it accurately reflects who they are and want to be. As a result, this discussion can take less than 30 minutes.

- **A longer conversation**: I have consulted with parishes that have not reviewed their vision or mission statement for some time. As a result, their core planning teams have decided the statements need to be reviewed and possibly modified. In these cases, I recommend discussing the following:
  - What do I like about the current vision or mission statement?
  - What do I not like about the statement?
  - What is missing from the current vision or mission statement?
  - What is God calling us to be?

After an hour or so of talking all this over, it can be helpful to have someone on the core planning team craft a few new statements. These can be reviewed by the team at a future meeting.

I have also had success asking each member of the team to come up with a version of a mission or vision statement and sharing it with the group. The group can discuss the different versions at another meeting. In addition, you might consider sharing the draft statements with members of the parish at listening sessions or staff meetings to gather input.

Although it can be tempting to try to create the "perfect" statement and agonize over every word, it is important to craft a statement that reflects your parish and something that the parish can support and live out. This should be completed within one to three meetings instead of dragging it out over several months.

Section 3

Assessing the
Current State

Chapter 6

Assessing the Current State through Data Collection, Listening, And Openness to the Holy Spirit

An important aspect of strategic planning is assessing the current state of the parish. It's common for many active members of the parish and even key staff members and volunteers to be unaware of the parish's finances, history, staffing structure or programs. This chapter focuses on ways to gather quantitative and qualitative data that will inform decision making.

Data Collection

The core planning team should identify the key data that's necessary for the planning process. While parishes may collect different types of information, I generally recommend compiling the following:

- Mass attendance over the last five years
- Membership over the last five years
- Tithing and other dollars raised over the last five years
- Programs offered and the number of participants
- Pertinent financial information, such as investments and major financial needs

- Staffing structure
- Active ministries and committees
- Major accomplishments
- Any pertinent changes

This information can be compiled into a "State of the Parish" report to be shared with the parish community. This is a great way to inform and educate parishioners. The report can be shared at the end of mass, through an online video presentation or at listening sessions. In order to set a future direction, it is helpful to understand the parish's current situation.

Listening

In addition to the data discussed in the last chapter, it's important to get input from the parish and community. This strategic planning process applies the spirit of synodality that emphasizes listening and learning.

Strategic planning is a wonderful opportunity to engage parishioners and non-parishioners. It's important to gather input from people of different ages, genders, backgrounds, races, ethnicities, and life stages, including those who have been involved with the parish for different lengths of time.

Many nonprofit organizations focus only on those with influence and affluence: Those able to financially support the organization and those who can influence others to support the organization. If you think an outcome of the strategic planning process is a major fundraising campaign, you will want to make sure some of your top prospective donors are engaged in the listening process. But this should never be done to the exclusion of parishioners.

It's important to be inclusive when going through the strategic planning process. We want to make sure that all people of God are welcomed into this process and given an opportunity to provide input. That is the spirit of synodality as described by Pope Francis.

Pros and Cons of Different Methods of Listening

There are a number of ways to gather input during the strategic planning process. Each has its advantages and disadvantages.

Surveys

Surveys are very inclusive and a great way to gather input from a lot of people. They are relatively easy to administer through online tools like SurveyMonkey and Google Forms. Many parishes can create and administer their own surveys, and these can be customized based on the type of feedback you're after.

You'll need to balance the length of time necessary to complete the survey with the depth of detail you want. In general, shorter surveys will receive more responses, but you may not receive all of the information you desire. Longer surveys will have a lower response rate, but the responses may be richer in details.

I recommend parish surveys include a SWOT analysis that asks respondents to identify the parish's internal **S**trengths, **W**eaknesses, external **O**pportunities, and **T**hreats:

1. What are the strengths of our parish?
2. What are our weaknesses?
3. What opportunities exist?
4. What threats do our parish face?

Another option is to ask questions based on the Diocese of Burlington synod:

1. What is our parish doing well?
2. What could we be doing better?
3. What is our parish not doing that we should do?

Ask respondents to prioritize items from the survey that should be part of the strategic plan. Some parishes ask for demographic information, such as age and length of membership in the parish. This information can help you decide if all demographic groups have been reached, but some people may not want to share this information, and that's OK. Online survey programs can also help break down responses by different demographics. For example, you might be interested in how responses compare between younger and older parishioners.

I recommend giving parishioners two to three weeks to complete a survey. In addition to getting feedback from those who attend your church, your parish might consider administering surveys to former parishioners, visitors and non-Catholics. Asking for input can be a great way to connect with non-parishioners. I suggest primarily focusing on online surveys, while also providing a paper survey option. Remember that 85% of Americans now own a smartphone, so providing a mobile-friendly survey should reach a high percentage of people. Some parishes have even distributed printed copies of surveys in the pew and asked parishioners to complete them.

One limitation of surveys is that you're not able to ask people immediate follow-up questions to get more context for responses. But using surveys in combination with listening sessions can provide you with that more dynamic understanding of feedback.

See also:
- Appendix C: Survey example (parishioner)
- Appendix D: Survey example (non-parishioner)

Group Listening Sessions

I highly recommend using group listening sessions. They provide excellent feedback and an opportunity for the facilitator to ask follow-up questions to clarify the meaning of responses.

You can accomplish a great deal in a two- to three-hour listening session. The main downside is that some people may not feel comfortable sharing dissenting opinions with the group. In these instances, I encourage the session attendees to provide this type of information in an anonymous survey.

Consider providing multiple listening sessions that are offered at various times of the day to accommodate different schedules. Providing in-person and virtual options helps remove barriers to attendance. Another option is hosting one large event in the evening or on a Saturday with multiple facilitators leading listening sessions. This can bring a lot of energy and excitement to a strategic planning process.

For a listening session to be effective, it's important to find a strong facilitator to lead the session. This person should be comfortable keeping the meeting on schedule, providing ground rules for the session, encouraging all attendees to actively participate, keeping their opinions to themselves, and asking follow-up questions to better understand the responses.

I find homogenous groups can help people feel more comfortable sharing. Your parish might consider individual listening sessions with staff members, new parishioners, longtime parishioners, young parents, youth, and parish council, for example. We need to be aware of power dynamics that could keep people from fully sharing feedback. For instance, new parishioners might not feel comfortable opening up with longtime parishioners about their frustrations.

Your parish might consider hosting multiple listening sessions and inviting specific people to each. Personal invitations are most effective for recruiting people to attend. The pastor or members of the core planning team can play a key role in inviting people through phone calls and personal outreach. In general, I think having an in-person group of fewer than 20 people helps ensure everyone has an opportunity to actively participate. Virtual meetings are most productive when they have twelve or fewer attendees. When groups are larger than that, you may have some people who ultimately don't contribute.

See also:
- Appendix E: Sample survey and listening session invitation letter
- Appendix F: Sample listening session agenda
- Appendix G: Sample listening session prayers

The pastor can lead a prayer or consider asking the group to recite "Come, Holy Spirit" (Appendix G lists sample prayers). The prayer should invoke the Holy Spirit and encourage the attendees to be attentive to the Spirit.

State of the Parish Presentation

This part of the program is optional but strongly encouraged. Communication is a challenge in most organizations, and parishes are no exception. This event can be an opportunity to inform parishioners of the current state of the parish.

I recommend a 10- to 15-minute presentation to communicate important information to parishioners that improves their understanding of the strategic issues facing the parish. This can be done by the pastor, staff, or members of the core planning team.

Facilitated SWOT Analysis

After the State of the Parish presentation, a facilitator should lead attendees through a SWOT analysis. Some pastors stay to listen to participants. Others feel like it's better for them to leave to ensure everyone feels comfortable sharing their opinions.

It is important to introduce some ground rules for the SWOT analysis discussion. These instructions will encourage attendees to feel comfortable sharing their honest feedback. The facilitator might say the following, for instance:

> We are gathered today to discuss the future of our parish. I am going to ask you questions about the parish, and it is important that you be as honest as possible. We are not going to use this session to debate, judge, or evaluate your responses. If you think something, please say it, and I will write it down. At the end of the session, I will ask you to identify the most important priorities for the strategic plan.

The facilitated SWOT analysis asks attendees these questions:
1.   What are the strengths of our parish?
2.   What are our weaknesses?
3.   What opportunities exist?
4.   What threats do our parish face?

The strengths and weaknesses should typically focus on internal aspects of the parish, while the latter two questions are about external opportunities and threats.

As an alternative to the SWOT analysis, you could instead ask the following questions that are based on the Diocese of Burlington's synod:
1.   What is our parish doing well?
2.   What could we be doing better?
3.   What is our parish *not* doing that we *should* do?

Have the facilitator ask the questions. Then that person or someone else can record the answers. I recommend using an easel with large sticky note flip chart paper and markers to write down all responses. You'll need a room with plenty of wall space as well. Once you've filled up your sheet with responses, tear it off and hang it on the wall for everyone to see. This ensures participants actually see their responses get written down, and that they feel heard.

It's best to record all of the responses for one question before moving on to the next one. However, you can always add responses for previous questions as needed. The facilitator should remain neutral and ensure others do as well in terms of sharing opinions and thoughts about someone else's responses. If someone disagrees with a statement, the facilitator should remind the group that we are not judging or evaluating ideas. When applicable, the facilitator can take note of what a group member disagrees with to make sure people are heard and handle any conflict in a productive way.

After responses for each question have been captured, the facilitator should thank everyone for their input and provide each attendee with stickers to select the responses that they feel are most important to include in the strategic plan. Color-coding label stickers (small circular stickers in various colors) work well and can be purchased at any office supply store. I typically provide attendees with about five stickers each. The attendees are then given approximately 10 minutes to place their stickers on the responses that they feel are most important to consider for the strategic plan. I sometimes view the stickers as an exclamation point that allows the group to take the pulse of the room.

Once all attendees have placed stickers on the responses, the facilitator can identify those responses that have a cluster of stickers. The facilitator should thank everyone for their input and let them know that the responses will be typed up and compiled with any other listening session responses. This information will help the core planning team determine priorities for the strategic plan.

After the session, someone should type up all responses written on the flip chart paper and include the number of stickers for each of the responses. I recommend categorizing similar responses and noting how many stickers were used for each theme. This should not be seen as a democratic process in which the greatest number of stickers results in the top priority. But it will help the core planning team understand perceived priorities from the parish.

For transparency, I recommend you thank the listening session attendees through an email or letter and send them a copy of the typed responses.

Interviews

Interviews are another great way to gather input. Members of the core planning team can serve as interviewers and identify people that are unable to attend the listening sessions or might feel more comfortable in a one-on-one conversation.

The downside to interviews is that they can be time-consuming and it's difficult to have consistency from one interviewer to the next. To help standardize the process, the same questions from the listening session can be used for interviews. All interview responses should be written down and included in an interview report. I suggest removing names from those who are interviewed in the report.

Virtual versus in-person

Parishes should consider using a combination of in-person and virtual meetings for listening sessions and interviews to reflect the shift toward increased digital communication. Virtual listening sessions can use the same format as the in-person session described above. In general, I think virtual meetings should be smaller in size (no more than 12 people) to ensure engagement of the participants.

Instead of using an easel and flipchart paper, a Word Document, Google Doc, or digital whiteboard can be shared on the screen so attendees can view the responses being written down. At the end of the session, the facilitator can ask everyone to share their top priorities with the group. Providing a link to access and edit the document for participants is also an option, though it can sometimes feel clunky. For this, I share a link to the document in the chat of Zoom or whatever platform I'm using and ask participants to place an exclamation point or symbol next to each of their top five priorities.

Another option is for the facilitator to email the document to all attendees after the meeting and ask them to reply with their top priorities within a couple of days. The facilitator can edit the document to show how many attendees identified responses as a priority.

Compiling the Report

At the end of the listening phase, all session notes and survey responses should be compiled in a single report that can be shared with the core planning team. It can be valuable to combine the responses into themes and share the number of people who selected that response or theme as a priority.

The core planning team can also choose to send copies of the report to listening session attendees or the entire parish to increase transparency during the planning process. Negative comments about individuals may need to be removed from the report out of respect for those people.

If done correctly, the report represents the experiences and feelings of the parish community. Members and nonmembers have had an opportunity to share their thoughts about the future of the parish.

Section 4

Plan Development

Chapter 7

Core Planning
Team Retreat

It is now time to begin developing the plan. The vision and mission statement and data collected through the listening phase should guide decision-making. As you start developing the plan, it's essential to be intentional about embedding the vision and mission throughout the planning process, plan development, and implementation.

The next step will be a half-day retreat for the core planning team. This meeting will allow the group to spend an extended period of time together reflecting on responses and discussing priorities for the parish. The retreat is a great way to engage the core planning team in high level, strategic thinking.

In advance of the retreat, core planning team members should receive listening session and survey reports and spend time reviewing the responses. In-person retreats are preferred, but parishes may also consider having virtual retreats to accommodate schedules and other constraints.

See also:
- Appendix H: Sample core planning team retreat agenda
- Appendix I: A Creative's Prayer

The "Come, Holy Spirit" prayer or an improvised prayer is appropriate for this meeting. Another option is "A Creative's Prayer" from www.catholiccreatives.com. This prayer is a nice way to encourage the group to really think differently. The goal of the prayer is to invite the Holy Spirit to be present and for the team members to open themselves to the Spirit.

Review Organizational Purpose

If your parish has not finalized your vision or mission statement, you should begin the retreat discussing and finalizing a version of the statement(s). This can be a difficult process because people sometimes get hung up on the specific wording. I recommend that planning teams work to ensure the spirit of the statement captures who the parish is and wants to be. Spending too much time on individual word preferences can be counterproductive.

Review Listening Reports

In the spirit of synodality, it's important for the core planning team to listen to and learn from the respondents. We might have a tendency to be defensive about some of the responses, but it is necessary to be open to the input of the community. Someone should serve as a facilitator for the group and ask the following questions:

1. What are the reports telling you?
2. What surprised you about the responses?
3. What new questions have the reports raised that you may want to explore in the future?
4. How aligned are members of the parish with each other?

I recommend the facilitator write down all of the responses on an easel with large flip chart paper to allow the attendees to see the input from the group.

Identifying Key Problems and Opportunities

In my work as a creative problem-solving facilitator, I learned to define problems and opportunities through the phrase "How might we ... ?" by Dr. Min Basadur. Basadur explained:

> People may start out asking, "How can we do this," or "How should we do that?" But as soon as you start using words like *can* and *should*, you're implying judgment: Can we really do it? And should we?" By substituting the word *might*, he says, "you're able to defer judgment, which helps people to create options more freely, and opens up more possibilities.[12]

The facilitator should ask the group to share "How might we ... ?" statements that identify problems to solve and opportunities to pursue. It may be necessary for the facilitator to provide an example, such as asking, "How might we increase mass attendance?" or "How might we utilize technology for faith formation?" The group should be encouraged to think divergently and list as many "How might we ... ?" responses as possible.

Many of the "How might we ... ?" items will directly relate to the themes that emerged during the listening phase. The facilitator should explain that there is no judgment right now, and the group will narrow down the choices after capturing responses from the group. All responses should be written down on the easel with flipchart paper.

Once the group has generated a good list of statements, the facilitator should ask the core planning team to select approximately three to five that they think need to be addressed in the strategic plan. Using the sticker method from the listening session—and giving each team member three dots to place on the "How might we ... ?" statements—can help quickly narrow these down.

After the stickers are placed, the group should discuss which items might be a focus of the strategic plan. If some are similar, they can be combined. For example, you might have multiple statements related to increasing members or engaging youth. This is a good time to remind everyone to be open to the Holy Spirit.

After the selections have been made, the facilitator might also ask, "Do these statements address the strategic issues impacting our parish?" or "What is God calling us to be as a parish?" I want to emphasize that this is not a democratic process where the responses with the most stickers automatically become priorities for the strategic plan. This is an important time to really reflect on key strategic issues, and it is ideal for the core planning team and pastor to reach a level of agreement.

I would recommend moving forward with three to five statements to spend further time discussing, clarifying, and developing. Having too many to consider can lead to a lack of focus for the strategic plan.

Small Group Work

Once the group has narrowed down the number of priorities to address, team members can break into small groups to discuss and begin adding detail to these strategic focus areas. Small groups should complete the strategic planning worksheet (Appendix J) without agonizing over the details. Remember, this is a preliminary discussion to begin developing aspects of the strategic plan.

The strategic planning worksheet includes the following:

- **"How might we ...?" statements:** Write in the priority "How might we ...?" items that the core planning team selected.
- **Owner:** This is the person responsible for accomplishing the stated objectives. Ideally, for this, you'll list the name of a person or position who will be responsible for implementing this part of the strategic plan. An owner can

be a staff member or volunteer. I caution groups against identifying committees as owners, since that often leads to a lack of follow-through, accountability, and commitment.

- **Team members:** Here you're spelling out who will help support these efforts. Identifying a committee or team to support the owner will help with accountability and implementation. The parish might have an existing committee that can help, such as a building and grounds committee, or a new committee may need to be created. Consider listing the names of specific parishioners who could help. This is a great way to engage parishioners' specific gifts and talents.

- **Desired outcome:** What do you really want to accomplish? How will you know you accomplished it? Begin with the end in mind. Spend some time writing a vivid description of what the favored outcome will look like. A paragraph is adequate.

- **Milestone objectives:** For this, you'll want to outline key measures for success in the first, second and third year, and so on. Measuring success in churches can be extremely difficult. In the past, most churches typically only measured three things: membership numbers, mass attendance, and collections. I encourage you to really think about clearly articulating your indicators for success to understand what you truly hope to accomplish. Clarifying these measures will help the parish work toward a specific goal. In addition, you will need to outline how you will collect data and measure progress.

- **Strategies and Initiatives (Year 1, Year 2, Year 3):** Having these clearly outlined will help you meet key performance metrics and ultimately achieve your desired outcomes. Consider the work that will need to take place.

- **Action Steps (Year 1, Year 2, Year 3):** Action steps break down the strategies and initiatives into bite-sized pieces.
- **Resources needed:** This may include budget dollars, staff resources, or assistance from an external source. Although it can be difficult to estimate a cost, it is advantageous to provide as much information now as possible.

Once the groups have had time to work together (around 30 to 45 minutes should be sufficient), they will briefly report their work to the full core planning team. Allow time for comments, suggestions, questions, and discussion. The recorder from each group can add comments from the group to their worksheet.

Retreat Closing

At the end of the retreat, the next steps should be discussed. Someone will need to type notes or draft an initial strategic plan based on the strategic planning worksheets. A strategic plan may be as simple as the example in Appendix K. If you are interested in a more detailed strategic plan template, you can find one in Appendix L.

Then the core planning team should discuss how information will be communicated to the parish community.

Chapter 8

Communicating the Initial Plan to Your Community

After the retreat, the core planning team will provide an update to the parish and invite parishioners to get involved with the implementation of the plan. The initial elements of the strategic plan will be shared with the parish for additional input.

Updates can come in the form of a letter, email, social media post, web page, mass announcement, or a combination of these. You should use multiple methods of communication and stress that the initial focus areas have been developed as a result of the feedback received from the parish and community. That way, it doesn't seem as if arbitrary decrees have come down from on high. Additionally, it's important to thank everyone for their input and time.

The core planning team might also schedule a meeting with the parish staff to get their feedback on the draft plan. Parishioners and staff should be asked: Is there anything missing? What concerns do you have? What part of the plan would you like to help with?

See also:
Appendix M: Sample strategic plan focus areas letter

The core planning team should meet to review any feedback received and identify volunteers who want to help and finalize the plan. If the core planning team is separate from the parish council, the team should provide an update to the parish council and ask for their input or affirmation. This is also an important time to ensure support for the initial plan from the pastor because he is ultimately the person who will approve the plan.

Chapter 9

Continuing to Develop the Strategic Plan

Although it is tempting to try to create the perfect strategic plan, it is most important to have a plan in place that represents the desired direction of the parish. Strategic plans should be viewed as works in progress that are living and breathing documents. They can be adjusted and adapted as needed. The time needed to make these changes will vary depending on the parish.

Some parishes choose to have their core planning team refine and finalize their strategic plan. If that is the case for your parish, then you can skip the "Task forces for further study" section. However, your parish may decide that additional input, study, and expertise are needed to develop the plan. In this case, creating task forces for further study can be helpful.

Task Forces for Further Study

After the initial priorities for the strategic plan have been identified, you may choose to form task forces around all or some of the strategic focus areas. This is a great opportunity to continue the path of synodality through listening and learning.

A volunteer chairperson should be selected to lead each task force. Task forces are a great way to engage new people within the parish community. A task force can be relatively small but should include parishioners or community members who are knowledgeable and passionate about that focus area.

The task forces can begin by reviewing the strategic planning worksheet created during the core planning team retreat or an initial strategic plan draft. They will determine what's needed to address the strategic focus area.

How much study is needed to make this judgment call will depend on the focus area. If the focus is maintenance of existing facilities, for example, then in a relatively short amount of time, the group can probably begin finalizing a timeline and identifying what needs to be accomplished. If the focus area is related to adding new facilities, the work of the task force will be more extensive as they identify everything from specific needs to costs and opportunities to raise funds.

Your parish may have parishioners with expertise in the selected focus areas. However, there will be times when your parish has a limited understanding of an issue, and a task force will be required to spend a great deal of time studying an issue to become more knowledgeable about it.

That's typically the case with increasing membership. The task force may need to study resources related to evangelization, attracting Catholics who have fallen away from the church, and marketing techniques, as well as what successful parishes have done to increase mass attendance and membership.

A book study may provide the information needed to inform the development of the plan by members reading about successes and recommendations from other parishes. If one of your focus areas is youth, a youth task force may choose to learn more by interviewing active and inactive young people in the parish to understand their needs and desires.

An example agenda for a first task force meeting includes these items:

- Opening prayer
- Review of the listening phase report (including survey and listening session responses)

- Review of the assigned strategic focus area (see your strategic planning worksheet or strategic plan draft)
- Discussion: What do we know about this strategic focus area? What do we *not* know about this strategic focus area?
- What resources are available to help us learn about what's needed?

Next Steps

After the meeting, the task force will report back to the core planning team with meeting notes. The core planning team should set a timeline for the task forces to meet and finalize input for the strategic plan. In general, this part of the process should last a month or two. The final task force report may be an expanded version of the strategic planning worksheet or updated strategic plan document. If needed, the core planning team may continue to ask the task force for input.

Once the task forces have met and submitted a final report to the core planning team, it's time to begin finalizing the strategic plan. The listening process continues as the core planning team reviews and learns from the task forces. The core planning team should be able to finalize the plan within one to three meetings.

In general, strategic plans should cover three to five years and be reviewed on a regular basis. The strategic plan should include the following at a minimum:

1. **Owner:** Who is responsible for the implementation for the strategic plan focus area? I recommend the name of a specific staff or volunteer position be listed for this.
2. **Team:** What team will support the owner in implementing each focus area? The team can be an existing committee or newly formed group.

3. **Objectives and outcomes:** What change do you desire to make as a result of this plan? This section should be measurable as much as possible. In addition, establishing timelines and setting deadlines will create urgency.
4. **Strategies:** What will the team do to achieve the desired objectives or outcomes? This section should be specific and include timelines.

See also:
- Appendix K: Simple strategic plan template

If this is your parish's first strategic planning process, I recommend using a simple format for the plan that is concise but understandable to all who read it. However, the core planning team may also consider creating a more detailed plan. As described in Appendix L, that would include these:

1. **Owner:** as described above
2. **Team:** as described above
3. **Vivid description:** It can be helpful for teams to develop a brief and precise description of what success in this focus area will look like. The description might be a couple of sentences or paragraphs.
4. **Outcome:** In this template, the outcome will detail a three-to-five-year goal. This goal should be measurable to the extent that's possible. For example, increase mass attendance from 300 in 2021 to 400 people in 2025.
5. **Milestone objectives:** This should break down the outcome into smaller, more manageable goals.
6. **Strategy and action steps:** Here you'll describe what you will do to achieve the goal. Although it is tempting to list many different strategies and action steps, it is necessary to be selective and pick those that will have the most impact.

Also, keep in mind that strategies and action steps may change or evolve over time.

The core planning team may decide to share drafts of the plan with the parish or staff to continue gathering input. The above formats are an attempt to simplify the process of developing a plan. You might decide to expand on one of the examples above or to create a simple plan that evolves, and add more details over time. There is no perfect one-size-fits-all plan. I encourage parishes to err on the side of beginning implementation of an imperfect plan, rather than making a futile attempt to perfect a plan before moving to action.

I recommend the parish council review the plan and advise the pastor to approve it. Along with being responsible for approving the plan, the pastor will be involved in communicating regarding what's in the plan and its implementation.

Section 5

Implementation

Chapter 10

Putting Your Plan into Practice

Although many parishes are initially intimidated by the prospect of creating a strategic plan, acting on it is the hard part. The rollout needs to include a strategy for communication and implementation. In my experience, these are areas that are often neglected.

Communication Plan

A central function of any strategic plan is communicating a vision for the future. The core planning team should work together to develop a plan for articulating the parish's vision. That means being intentional about keeping parishioners informed during this exciting time as the plan is rolled out and when progress occurs.

The core planning team should identify stakeholders who will receive information about the strategic plan, such as parishioners, visitors, community partners, and the diocese. There should be a meeting with the staff to share the plan and to help them understand how they will be involved.

Along with keeping parishioners informed, the core planning team should consider communicating to the community at large through social media, the parish's website, bulletins, mass announcements, and press releases. If a new initiative will appeal to the broader community, it will be important to broadcast this. Catholic parishes often err on the side of not communicating beyond the parish. Consider new ways to spread the word about your parish and its initiatives. You have an opportunity to create excitement and reach new people.

See also:
Appendix N: Communication rollout plan template

In addition to the rollout, the core planning team should consider how to communicate ongoing updates to the parish and greater community. This task often falls to the parish council, who will regularly review strategic plan progress. People appreciate hearing about progress, and this can include updates on successes, accomplishments, revision of the plan due to new circumstances, the need for help, and barriers to success. This communication should come at least annually, but short, more frequent updates are also effective.

See also:
Appendix O: Ongoing communication plan template

Creating Focus Area Teams

Focus area teams need to be formed to ensure implementation of the plan. The team might include members of task forces, but you can also consider expanding it to others as well. Team members should possess special knowledge or experiences that will advance the focus area. Most importantly, they must be passionate about that focus area and be committed to helping. The size of the team will depend on the topic, but generally you'll want to have six to eight members.

To ensure successful functioning teams, it can be helpful to host an initial meeting or training session. This will communicate the vision and strategic plan components, and outline the expectations for focus area chairs and team members. The meeting might include only chairs, but you can also consider having a retreat with all team members to help them better understand their role and how that relates to the entire strategic plan.

Focus area teams should meet regularly. At the beginning of implementation, the teams will generally meet monthly or every other month to help with work, problem solve and provide input. Team members may be added as things progress or another perspective is needed.

Monitoring Implementation

I often say that creating a plan is the easy part of strategic planning. Implementation is much more difficult. For that reason, the core planning team should prioritize determining how the parish will move forward with a strategic plan.

Once the implementation begins, I recommend the parish council be responsible for overseeing the strategic plan. The parish council can also decide when it makes sense to provide updates, and make these a feature of regular meetings. For example, if your parish has four strategic plan focus areas, and your parish council meets nine times a year, you might review two of the focus areas, and where things stand with those, at each meeting. Then at the ninth or final meeting, you can do an annual review of the plan, and set goals for the upcoming year. Communicating this schedule to all focus area teams at the beginning of the year is a great way to ensure they are meeting regularly, making progress, and having some accountability.

This will help your parish stay on task with the implementation of the strategic plan while looking ahead. Many parish council meetings are focused on what has happened in the past, and I encourage them to instead be focused on the future. The strategic plan should be viewed as a living, breathing document. There are times when circumstances change, and it is necessary to adjust the plan or timeline accordingly. It's perfectly normal to adapt a plan.

The annual review can be a longer meeting to focus on what's been accomplished in the last year and what needs to be done in the next year. This meeting should include members of the parish council and possibly the focus area teams.

Implementation Reports

At designated parish council meetings, the focus area owner should provide a written update that indicates progress, next steps, significant changes in the plan since the last update, and challenges the team is facing. An example of an implementation template is outlined in Appendix P, and this type of report can be modified based on the needs of the parish. The parish council should discuss this focus area. The group can affirm the desired outcomes, make suggestions, or identify new resources.

See also:
Appendix P: Implementation template

The roles of parish council members and staff will vary depending on the parish. In larger parishes with more staff, it may be beneficial to assign a person who works for the church to help implement specific focus areas. But this may not be possible with smaller parishes. In either case, the parish council should review progress of the strategic plan's implementation on a regular basis.

Being Nimble in a Changing World

Our world is changing more rapidly than ever. As a result, we need to be able to adapt our strategic plans as necessary. The parish council or focus area team may also realize a portion of the plan document has not been clearly written or is no longer relevant, or that the strategic plan needs to be adapted for another reason. To modify the plan, I recommend the focus area team makes a recommendation for a change to the parish council. The parish council can advise the pastor to approve a change to the plan.

Section 6

Closing Thoughts and Resources

Chapter 11

Lessons Learned

By this point, I hope you feel knowledgeable enough about parish strategic planning to at least begin taking the first steps in the process. For review, here are some things worth considering to put the lessons you've learned into practice:

1. Strategic planning is a wonderful tool for engagement. This process provides parishes with an opportunity to invite people to provide input. When people feel like they are being listened to, they are more likely to feel positive about the parish and get involved.

2. Err on the side of involving too many in the process. As your parish gathers input, cast a wide net. Reach out to former parishioners, those in the church who are disengaged, visitors who attend mass but have not registered as parishioners, fallen-away Catholics, non-Catholics, and other community members. This is a great opportunity to personally invite people to get involved. All you're asking for is their time and opinions.

3. Strategic planning establishes and communicates a common purpose, vision, and priorities. The plan articulates a parish's priorities to parishioners, staff members, and the community. There are always too many ideas for a parish to implement, and the strategic planning process helps identify the most important priorities to devote time and resources to.

4. Utilize this process to consolidate your future-focused plans in a single document. It's common for parishes to have multiple plans that cover programs, facilities, and other areas. A strategic plan is one comprehensive document that centralizes your parish's vision so it can be more easily shared with parishioners and the greater community.

5. The process described in this book is designed to gain shared commitment to goals and strategies. There are multiple opportunities for involvement, sharing input, listening, and learning. Remember that much of the process involves building consensus around key strategic issues and solutions for addressing them.

6. When people understand the parish's priorities, and clear goals are identified, people will work together to accomplish the goals. That's why this process is so helpful not only to decide what you want to do as a parish but to be successful in achieving your objectives.

7. Whenever possible, make sure the goals you establish are measurable. Although it can be difficult to gauge success for a parish, there are ways to do this. Parishes who want to improve stewardship can set measurable goals such as dollars raised or percentage of parishioners who donate at a specific dollar amount.

8. Planning is easier than implementation. Many parishes feel uncomfortable working on a strategic planning process. They worry about how to put the plan document into the correct format. Plans look different based on the needs of the parish or organization. Although the planning process is time intensive, the most important and difficult work is the implementation of the plan.

9. Encourage creativity and dream big. People will naturally base their plans on previous experiences. But the past may not be the best guide for the future. Reflect on whether

incremental or transformational change is necessary to reach the desired results.

10. Synodality ensures planning is rooted in listening to one another and being open to the Holy Spirit. The Body of Christ includes all of God's people, not just the pastor, staff and active parishioners. Through a synodal process, we open ourselves to listen to God's call and learn from the experiences and thoughts of all people. In addition, this process helps build buy-in from those who are involved with providing input, developing the plan and implementing it.

Closing Thoughts

As Catholics, we believe that Jesus's death on the cross and resurrection secured our eternal life. In Matt Maher's song, "Christ is Risen," he encourages us to come stand in the light of Christ because our God is alive.

It is my prayer that the listening, learning, and responding that occurs through the path of synodality will result in our parishes being more alive than ever before. As we become more attentive to the Holy Spirit and develop and implement plans for the future of our parishes, let us ensure that our thoughts, words, and actions reflect an Easter people that proclaims, "He's alive!" This mindset will lead to more vibrant and engaged parishes committed to spreading the Gospel.

Addendum

Other Resources

My background includes training as a creative problem-solving process facilitator in the Basadur Simplexity Thinking process. One of the key ingredients of creativity and innovation is the ability to separate divergent thinking from convergent thinking. Many meetings involve mixing these two types of thinking.

There is tremendous value in gathering ideas or input before spending time evaluating or judging them. The SWOT analysis and "How might we . . . ?" exercises are based on divergent and convergent thinking. This process will help encourage creativity and active participation.

Change Management

John Kotter's book *Leading Change* (2012) is considered a classic on organizational change management. Parish leaders can benefit from reflecting on his eight-step process for creating change to ensure the success of the strategic plan. Your core planning team might utilize this resource to understand how to successfully navigate change. For example, the first step of the change management process is "Establishing a sense of urgency."

Kotter shares an example of a clear and focused vision from a business, and this description can help you understand what a vision might look like:

> The vision driving our department's reengineering
> effort is simple. We want to reduce our costs by at

least 30 percent and increase the speed with which we can respond to customers by at least 40 percent. These are stretch goals, but we know based on the pilot project in Austin that they are achievable if we all work together. When this is completed, in approximately three years, we will have leapfrogged our biggest competitors and achieved all the associated benefits: better customers, increased revenue growth, more job security, and the enormous pride that comes from great accomplishments.

If your team is looking for some good resources related to strategic planning, I recommend the following:

The 4 Disciplines of Execution: How to Achieve Your Wildly Important Goals by Chris McChesney, Sean Covey, and Jim Huling. Free Press.

- This book is great for setting goals and following through. This process includes identification of a "Wildly Important Goal" and weekly check-in meetings to ensure implementation and accountability. Many businesses and organizations have implemented 4DX.

Measure What Matters: How Google, Bono, and the Gates Foundation Rock the World with OKRs by John Doerr. Portfolio/Penguin.

- Doerr explains the process of Objectives and Key Results (OKRs) that has been used by Google and many other organizations. This process helps organizations identify and track what is most important to them.

Building Your Company's Vision by Jim Collins and Jerry Porras. Harvard Business Review.

- This is a classic strategy article that explains core purpose and values, and how to set BHAGs (Big, Hairy, Audacious Goals).

On Strategy. Harvard Business Review's 10 Must Reads.

- The cover reads: "If you read nothing else on strategy, read these definitive articles from *Harvard Business Review*." This collection of articles will provide excellent insights about strategy.

The Nonprofit Strategy Revolution: Real-Time Strategic Planning in a Rapid Response World (2nd Edition) by David LaPiana with Melissa Mendes Campos. Turner.

- This book provides nonprofits with a defined process for creating a business plan. The authors approach organizational, programmatic and operational strategy through this process.

FAQs

Q. How far into the future should a strategic plan look?

A. In general, I think a strategic plan can realistically look a maximum of three to five years in the future. Three years is probably more realistic, especially as we continue to experience rapid change in our world. A three-year plan can then be reviewed and revised each year as necessary. Some nonprofits are creating two-to-three-year plans and developing a one-year action plan each year as they make progress.

Q. How many strategic focus areas should be in a strategic plan?

A. This is a common question, and the answer depends on the types of goals selected. Parishes that select fewer goals will typically accomplish them compared to parishes that have multiple goals. It is common for parishes to select too much to focus on. Three to four focus areas seem to be realistic to successfully implement. When your parish is finalizing the plan, you should discuss whether you have the necessary resources to follow through with the plan.

Q. What happens if we can't find an owner for the strategic focus area?

A. If your core planning team cannot find an owner, that might mean there is a lack of sufficient interest and energy to support the priority. The planning team might have to consider whether the strategic focus area will remain a part of the plan. Be sure to fully explore possible owners in the parish. Many parishes have members with untapped talent who are waiting for a personal invitation to get involved.

Q. What is the difference between strategic planning and pastoral planning?

A. The phrases strategic planning and pastoral planning are sometimes used interchangeably. Pastoral planning helps parishes determine spiritual goals and typically does not involve goals related to finances, facilities, or other non-spiritual goals. Strategic planning can include spiritual and non-spiritual goals. The process in this book could be used for both planning types, but I have decided to focus on strategic planning because many parishes have both spiritual and non-spiritual planning needs.

Q. How do parishes with schools incorporate schools into a strategic planning process?

A. For parishes with a school, the school is a significant ministry and commitment of the parish. The school should be included in the strategic planning process, and I have seen this coordinated in several different ways. Parishes with schools often include school parents or other representatives on the core planning team. It can be helpful to host listening sessions specifically for school parents and staff. In addition, aspects of the school can become a specific focus area for the plan. Some parishes create task forces to further study school-specific issues. I have also seen parishes complete their own strategic planning process and then have a separate planning process for the school to align plans and implementation.

References

Allen, Jr., J. L. (2020, Feb. 23). *Pope to US bishops: No, 'synodality' doesn't mean 'democracy.'* Crux. https: //cruxnow.com/news-analysis/2020/02/pope-to-us-bishops-no-synodality-doesnt-mean-democracy/

Berger, W. (2012, Sept. 17). *The secret phrase top innovators use.* Harvard Business Review. https: //hbr.org/2012/09/the-secret-phrase-top-innovato

Bryson, J. M. (2018). *Strategic planning for public and nonprofit organizations: A guide to strengthening and sustaining organizational achievement* (5th ed.). Wiley.

Catholic Creatives. (n.d.). *A creative's prayer.* https: // catholiccreatives.com/prayer

Cernuzio, S. (2021, May 21). *Synod of Bishops will begin in the local Churches.* Vatican News. https: //www.vaticannews.va/en/pope/news/2021–05/synod-of-bishops-will-begin-in-the-local-churches.html

Collins, J. C., & Porras, J. I. (1996, Sept.). *Building your company's vision.* In *On Strategy* (pp. 77–102). Harvard Business Review.

Diocese of Burlington. (n.d.). *2018 synod.* https: //vermontcatholic. org/about/who-we-are/synod/

Diocese of San Diego. (n.d.). *Young adult synod.* https: // www.sdcatholic.org/office-for/young-adult-ministry/young-adult-synod/

General Secretariat for Synod of Bishops. (2021, Sept.). *Vademecum.* http://www.synod.va/en/documents/vademecum.html

Hansen, L. (2019, Sept. 12). *In the Amazon, Pope Francis is setting the agenda for a new kind of synod.* America: The Jesuit Review. https: //www.americamagazine.org/faith/2019/09/12/amazon-pope-francis-setting-agenda-new-kind-synod

Holy See Press Office. (2021, Sept. 9). *Preparatory Document for the 16th Ordinary General Assembly of the Synod of Bishops.* https://press.vatican.va/content/salastampa/en/bollettino/pubblico/2021/09/07/210907a.html

McChesney, C., Covey, S., Huling, J. (2012). *The 4 disciplines of execution: Achieving your wildly important goals.* Free Press.

Mobile fact sheet. (2021, Apr. 7). Pew Research Center. https: //www.pewresearch.org/internet/factsheet/mobile/

Pope Francis. (2015, Oct. 17). *Ceremony commemorating the 50th anniversary of the institution of the Synod of Bishops: Address of His Holiness Pope Francis.* http: //www.vatican.va/content/francesco/en/speeches/2015/october/documents/papa-francesco_20151017_50-anniversario-sinodo.html

Wooden, C. (2015, Oct. 17). *Pope calls for 'synodal' church that listens, learns, shares mission.* National Catholic Reporter. https: //www.ncronline.org/news/vatican/pope-calls-synodal-church-listens-learns-shares-mission

About the Author

Dr. Tad Dickel is a strategy, leadership, and creativity consultant who serves as president of T. A. Dickel Group, LLC. He specializes in strategic planning, leadership coaching, and creative problem-solving, and he works with a wide variety of organizations.

With a career that began in education, Tad has served as a Catholic high school president, principal, and teacher. He regularly teaches graduate courses in strategic planning, leadership, and school finance at Creighton University (Omaha, Nebraska) and University of Evansville (Indiana). Tad has presented at national, state, and local conferences and meetings about strategic planning, nonprofit board development, and planned giving.

Tad holds a PhD in educational leadership from Indiana State University. He earned a Certificate in Catholic School Leadership from Creighton University, a Certificate in Nonprofit Board Consulting from BoardSource, a Certificate in Fundraising Management from The Fund Raising School, a Certificate in Family Business Advising from the Family Firm Institute, and a Foundations in Design Thinking Certificate from IDEO U. He is also a Certified Basadur Simplexity Thinking Facilitator and Trainer, Certified Basadur Innovation Profile Administrator, and a Myers-Briggs Type Indicator (MBTI®) Certified Practitioner.

Tad resides in Evansville, Indiana, with his wife Andrea, a Catholic elementary school principal. They have four children and belong to Holy Redeemer Catholic Church.

Want to work with Tad? He is available for consulting, speaking, and coaching. He can be reached at tad@tadickel.com.

Appendix A

Strategic Planning Checklist

Task	Complete	In progress	N/A
Chapter 1-3			
Determine your parish's need for a strategic planning process.			
Decide whether this is an opportune time for it.			
Chapter 4			
Develop buy-in for a strategic planning process from the pastor.			
Develop buy-in from the lay leadership (may include parish council, finance council, and staff).			
Establish a core planning team.			
Create a conceptual agreement for the planning process that includes who will be involved and a timeline.			
Decide whether your team has the time and ability to successfully lead a strategic planning process or if some external resources will be needed.			
Communicate to the parish the process and how they can be involved.			
Chapter 5			
Review the parish vision/mission statements, and determine whether any changes need to be made.			

Chapter 6			
Collect pertinent data about the parish to inform the planning process.			
Compile data into a "State of the Parish" presentation.			
Identify how your parish will conduct the listening phase including who will be involved, how you will invite their participation, what questions to ask, how you will collect their input, and a timeline for this phase.			
Design and administer parish survey.			
Design and conduct listening sessions and/or interviews.			
Compile the listening phase report to include surveys, listening sessions, and/or interview input and provide to core planning team.			
Chapter 7			
Plan the core planning team retreat.			
Conduct the core planning team retreat.			
Finalize parish vision/mission statement.			
Complete the strategic planning worksheets with preliminary plan elements.			
Chapter 8			
Communicate the initial plan priorities to the parish community and ask for feedback and interest in volunteering to help.			
Review feedback from parish and volunteers willing to help.			
Ensure support for the initial plan from the pastor.			
Ensure support for the initial plan from the parish council and finance council.			
Chapter 9			
Develop task forces to study the focus areas and provide additional input for the core planning team.			

Task forces meet and provide a report for the core planning team.			
Review task force input.			
Core planning team develops and finalizes the proposed strategic plan.			
Receive support for plan from lay leadership including parish council, finance council, and staff.			
Approval from pastor for the strategic plan.			
Chapter 10			
Communicate final plan to the parish and community.			
Develop an implementation plan and schedule for reviewing progress at parish council meetings.			
Create focus area teams with chairs.			
Review and revise plan as necessary.			
Ongoing communication to parish and community with progress updates.			

Appendix B

Sample Letter to Parish Introducing the Strategic Planning Process

Note: This letter should be modified to meet your parish's unique needs and character.

Dear Parishioners,

Over the last few months, I have engaged in conversation about the future direction of our parish with members of the parish council, parishioners, staff members, and others who are knowledgeable about planning processes. We think a long-term planning process is necessary for several reasons [list reasons below]:

The planning committee is excited to move forward with a planning process for our parish. We sincerely hope that all members of our parish community will participate in this process. As we begin this planning process, we ask for your prayers as we develop a vision for the future of our parish.

The first step of the process will include an opportunity for us to listen. All members of our parish community are invited to provide input through a survey. Please look for a link to the survey in an email and in the weekly parish bulletin. In addition, we will have paper copies of the surveys available in the parish office. Please complete all surveys no later than [insert date].

We would also like to gather input from those who do not regularly attend church. We are asking you to invite three friends, family members, or neighbors who do not attend a church to complete a different survey. The survey should take less than 10 minutes, and we think this input will be valuable for our future efforts. We would like these surveys completed by [insert date].

Based on your feedback, we hope to create a parish plan for the upcoming 3–5 years. Your involvement in this process will help us ensure a vibrant future and renewed sense of mission at our parish. I sincerely appreciate your prayers and willingness to support this important effort.

Blessings,
[Insert Name],
Pastor

Appendix C
Survey Example (Parishioner)

Directions: Please respond to the following questions that will inform the parish planning process. Your honest and candid responses are greatly appreciated.

1. What are the greatest strengths of [insert name] Parish?

   _____

   _____

2. What are the greatest weaknesses of our parish?

   _____

   _____

3. What are our greatest opportunities for improvement or change?

   _____

   _____

4. What are the greatest threats for the future of [insert name] Parish?

   _____

   _____

5. What are three to five priorities that the parish needs to focus on over the next three to five years?

_____

_____

6. Of the priorities you identified, which *one* would you be interested in volunteering your time and talent to support?

_____

_____

7. What other information do you think is important for us to consider as we begin this planning process?

_____

_____

8. Are you a registered member of the parish? (Circle one.)
   Yes   No   Not sure

9. If you are a registered member of the parish, how long have you been a member? (Circle one.)
   a. Parishioner for 5 years or less.
   b. Parishioner for 6–10 years.
   c. Parishioner for 11–15 years.
   d. Parishioner for 16–20 years
   e. Parishioner for more than 20 years.

10. If you are not a registered member, please consider leaving your name and contact information below for follow up.

Please return to the parish no later than [insert date].

Appendix D

Survey Example (Non-Parishioner)

Non-Parishioner Survey

Please respond to the following questions to help us better serve the needs of the community.

1. Age
   a. Under 18 years old
   b. 18–24 years old
   c. 25–34 years old
   d. 35–44 years old
   e. 45–54 years old
   f. 55–64 years old
   g. 65–74 years old
   h. 75 years or older

2. Please select the phrase that best describes you.
   a. Current practicing Catholic
   b. Former Catholic
   c. Christian but not Catholic
   d. Religious—Non-Christian religion
   e. Spiritual but not affiliated with a church
   f. Not religious/spiritual

3. How did you hear about (insert parish name)?
   a. Social media
   b. Word of mouth from friend or relative
   c. Living in the neighborhood
   d. Other (please explain)

4. Please select the response that best describes you.
   a. I have never regularly attended a church.
   b. I used to attend church regularly.
   c. I occasionally attend a church.
   d. I regularly attend another church.
   e. I regularly attend [insert parish name].

5. If you previously attended a church, why did you stop? (Please explain.)

6. If you do not currently attend a church, what would interest you in joining one?
   a. Welcoming atmosphere
   b. Opportunities to serve the poor
   c. Prayer groups
   d. Bible studies
   e. Social events
   f. Other (please explain)

7. Because of our specific location and facilities, what solutions and opportunities could we provide that no other church in our area can do as well?

8. Would you like more information about our church? (Yes/No)
   a. If so, please leave your name, phone number, and email address below.

Appendix E:

Sample Survey and Listening Session Invitation Letter

Dear Parishioners,

Greetings from [insert name] Parish. In recent months, the parish council has recognized the importance of long-term planning for our parish. We are beginning a strategic planning process and need your help. I believe long-term planning is an important next step to look at where we are and where we want to go as a parish family.

The first step of the process will include listening, and the parish council would like your input through a survey *or* listening sessions that will be conducted virtually and in person. A survey is included with this letter. You can complete the survey and mail it to or drop it off at the parish office, or you can complete it online through the following link: [insert link]. The deadline for completing surveys is [insert date].

In case you would prefer to attend a virtual or in-person listening session, here is a listing of the scheduled meetings:

- Thursday, February 18: 9:00–11:00 AM (in person) at [insert location]Thursday,

February 18: 6:00–8:00 PM (virtual) Zoom link:
[insert link]

- Tuesday, February 23: 9:00–11:00 AM (virtual) Zoom link: [insert link]
- Tuesday, February 23: 6:00–8:00 PM (in person) at [insert location]The virtual sessions will take place on Zoom. For the in-person sessions, we will conduct them in the parish hall.

Based on your feedback, we will create a strategic plan for the upcoming 3–5 years. If you have any questions, please contact me. Your involvement in this process will help us ensure a vibrant future and renewed sense of mission for our parish. I sincerely appreciate your consideration and look forward to hearing from you.

Faithfully yours,
[Insert Name],
Pastor

Appendix F

Sample Listening Session Agenda

Listening Session Agenda
[insert date]

Opening Prayer—5 minutes

Introductions—5 minutes

State of the Parish Presentation—15 minutes

SWOT Analysis—80 minutes

1. What are the strengths of our parish?
2. What are our weaknesses?
3. What opportunities exist?
4. What threats do our parish face?

Select key priorities for the strategic plan—10 minutes

Review key priorities—5 minutes

Adjourn meeting

Appendix G

Sample Listening Session Prayers

"Come, Holy Spirit"

Come, Holy Spirit, fill the hearts of your faithful and kindle in them the fire of your love. Send forth your Spirit, and they shall be created. And You shall renew the face of the earth.

O, God, who by the light of the Holy Spirit did instruct the hearts of the faithful, grant that by the same Holy Spirit we may be truly wise and ever enjoy His consolations, Through Christ Our Lord, Amen.

Sample Prayer:

Creator of the universe,

Thank you for bringing us together to discern the future of [insert name] parish. We are grateful for the many people who give generously of their time, talent, and treasure to help us build your kingdom.

May we open our hearts and minds to your will as we invite the Holy Spirit to guide us in our discussions and deliberations. May this session be a time we be a productive opportunity to listen and learn from our brothers and sisters in Christ.

May all that we say and do bring glory and honor to your holy name. We ask this in the name of your Son, Jesus Christ our Lord. Amen."

"Open My Eyes, Lord"©1988, 1998

Jesse Manibusan. Published by Spirit & Song® a division of OCP.

This song encourages us to be open to what God wants us to see, hear, and feel.

Appendix H

Sample Core Planning Team Retreat Agenda

Core Planning Team Retreat Agenda
(insert date)
Opening Prayer—5 minutes

Review organizational purpose—30 minutes

Review listening reports—30 minutes

1. What are the reports telling you?
2. What surprised you about the responses?
3. How aligned are members of the parish with each other?

Select key priorities for the strategic plan—10 minutes

Break—10 minutes

Select key "How might we ... ?" statements—30 minutes

Small group work—30 minutes
• Complete Appendix J: Strategic planning worksheet

Share small group work with the full group—30 minutes

Next steps and next meeting—30 minutes

A Creative's Prayer

Creator of the Universe, how infinite

And astonishing are your worlds.

O Divine Imagination, you created a creator

When you imagined me into existence.

Breathe breath into so much dust.

Let me lament for forgetting daily

To rise up out of the clay.

Free me from the deceit of the mundane,

And from the lure of comfort

Which dulls all of my given edges.

Most of all, Light of my life,

Forgive my blindness, open all my eyes,

Salt me with newness and dreams.

Fire my soul with your inventive flame,

Let me be committed to the world by it,

And find in it the deepest joy.

Universal Creativity, flow through me,

Faith to see things not yet seen,

Hope to overflow broken cisterns,

And Love to free me forever.

Flow, Oh river, from the Holy Temple,

Through my mind to my hand.

Infuse my work with spirit,

To feed hungry souls.

From Catholic Creatives (https: //catholiccreatives.com/prayer)

Appendix J

Strategic Planning Worksheet

How might we...? statement:
Owner (Who will be responsible for accomplishing this?):

_____

_____

Team members (Who will help support these efforts?)

_____

_____

3-5 Year Desired Outcome (What do you really want to accomplish? How will you know you accomplished it?):

_____

_____

_____

_____

Milestone objectives (What are key measures for success in Year 1, Year 2, Year 3, etc.?):

_____

_____

_____

_____

Strategies/Initiatives (Year 1, Year 2, Year 3):

_____

_____

_____

_____

Action Steps (Year 1, Year 2, Year 3):

_____

_____

_____

_____

Resources needed:

_____

_____

_____

_____

Appendix K

Simple Strategic Plan Template

Strategic Focus Area #1:

Owner:

Team:

Objectives:

Strategies:

More Detailed Strategic Plan Template

Strategic Focus Area #1:

Owner:

Team:

Vivid description:
Outcome:
Milestone Objective #1:
- Strategy/Action Steps:

    a.

Milestone Objective #2:
- Strategy/Action Steps:

    a.

Milestone Objective #3:
- Strategy/Action Steps:
    a.

Appendix M

Sample Strategic Plan Focus Areas Letter

Note to reader: Adapt this letter as needed, inserting correct information in the brackets, and changing the numbered items to match your parish's situation.

Dear [insert parish name] parishioner,

I am excited to provide you with an update on our parish planning process. You may recall this process began in [insert month] with a listening phase that included a survey that was emailed to parishioners and invitations to attend listening sessions. We received [insert number] survey responses, and [insert number] people attended the listening sessions. Thank you to everyone who provided their feedback.

Based on your input, we have developed three focus areas for the parish in the coming years. We are excited to share these focus areas and will continue to develop our vision for the future of [insert parish name]:

1. Marketing to prospective members: During the listening phase, many expressed concerns about membership. We have experienced a membership decline for the past five years, and we are hoping this plan will help us focus on increasing membership and mass attendance. A marketing committee will be developed to support these efforts.

2. Outreach to the poor: Our parishioners are passionate about helping the poor. An outreach committee will be created to coordinate efforts to include more parishioners in our outreach and to serve more less fortunate individuals in our community. Outreach may also be a way to engage young families and nonmembers of our parish.

3. Preserving our facilities: Our parish is blessed with beautiful but aging facilities. We desire to preserve our facilities by developing a long-term plan for their maintenance and also identify costs. The Buildings and Grounds Committee will be responsible for this important area.

We are excited to begin work on this plan. To achieve this vision, we need you to be involved. How can you help in this effort? If you are interested in getting involved with one of the committees, please let me know.

I would like to thank the core planning team for their leadership during this planning process: [insert names]. In addition, I want to thank our staff for their input and assistance: [insert names]. Thank you for your support and prayers.

Blessings,

[Insert Name]Pastor

Appendix N

Communication Roll Out Plan Template

Audience	Type of communication	Date	Who is responsible?
Staff	Staff meeting	[insert date]	The pastor will schedule the meeting and discuss the strategic plan with all staff.
Parishioners	Mass announcements	[insert date]	The parish council chair will write and deliver announcements at all weekend masses.
Parishioners	Bulletin announcement	[insert date]	The core planning team chair will write the announcement and provide to the parish secretary for the bulletin.
Parishioners	Letter to all parishioners	[insert date]	The pastor will write a letter for all parishioners and send it to the parish council for review. After the review, the pastor will have the parish secretary mail it to all parishioners.
Parishioners	Website	[insert date]	The pastor will include the letter to all parishioners and a copy of the strategic plan on the parish website.

Parishioners	Facebook page	[insert date]	The core planning team chair will send the strategic planning bulletin announcement to the social media coordinator and include a link to the strategic plan web page.
Greater Community	Website	[insert date]	The pastor will include the letter to all parishioners and a copy of the strategic plan on the parish website.
Greater Community	Facebook page	[insert date]	The core planning team chair will send the strategic planning bulletin announcement to the social media coordinator and include a link to the strategic plan web page.
Greater Community	Press Release	[insert date]	The parish council chair will create a press release and send to all local media about elements of the strategic plan.

Appendix O

Ongoing Communication Plan Template

Audience	Type of communication	Date	Who is responsible?
Staff	Staff meetings	[insert dates: first Wednesday of the quarter]	The pastor will discuss implementation of the strategic plan at quarterly staff meetings.
Parishioners	Mass announcements	[insert date: first weekend of each quarter]	The parish council chair will provide quarterly updates to the parish at all weekend masses.
Parishioners	Bulletin announcement	[insert date: first weekend of each quarter]	The parish council chair will provide a brief update in bulletins. The parish secretary will include in the bulletin.
Parishioners	Letter to all parishioners	[insert date: each year in May]	The pastor will write a letter to provide updates, successes, and challenges related to the strategic plan. The parish secretary will mail the letter to all parishioners.
Parishioners	Website	[insert date]	The pastor will include the update letter to all parishioners and a copy of the revised strategic plan on the parish website.

Parishioners	Facebook page	[insert date]	The core planning team chair will send the strategic planning bulletin announcement to the social media coordinator and include a link to the strategic plan web page.
Greater Community	Website	[insert date]	The pastor will include the update letter to all parishioners and a copy of the revised strategic plan on the parish website.
Greater Community	Facebook page	[insert date]	The core planning team chair will send the strategic planning bulletin announcement to the social media coordinator and include a link to the strategic plan web page.
Greater Community	Press Release	[insert date]	The parish council chair will create a press release and send to all local media about elements of the strategic plan.

Implementation Template

Strategic Focus Area #1:
Owner:
Team:

Objective	Owner	Timeline	Complete	Progress	Not started	Revise	Remove	Notes

Strategy	Owner	Timeline	Complete	Progress	Not started	Revise	Remove	Notes

Endnotes

1. Bryson, J. M. (2018). *Strategic planning for public and nonprofit organizations: A guide to strengthening and sustaining organizational achievement* (5th ed.). Wiley.

2. Wooden, C. (2015, Oct. 17). *Pope calls for "synodal" church that listens, learns, shares mission.* National Catholic Reporter. https: //www. ncronline.org/news/vatican/pope-calls-synodal-church-listens-learns-shares-mission

3. Pope Francis. (2015, Oct. 17). *Ceremony commemorating the 50th anniversary of the institution of the Synod of Bishops: Address of His Holiness Pope Francis.* http: //www.vatican.va/content/francesco/en/speeches/ 2015/october/documents/papa-francesco_20151017_50-anniversario-sinodo.html

4. Cernuzio, S. (2021, May 21). *Synod of Bishops will begin in the local Churches.* Vatican News. https: //www.vaticannews.va/en/pope/news/ 2021–05/synod-of-bishops-will-begin-in-the-local-churches.html

5. Diocese of Burlington. (n.d.). *2018 synod.* Retrieved April 9, 2021, https: //vermontcatholic.org/about/who-we-are/synod/

6. Diocese of San Diego. (n.d.). *Young adult synod.* Retrieved April 9, 2021, https://www.sdcatholic.org/office-for/young-adult-ministry/young-adult-synod/

7. Hansen, L. (2019, Sept. 12). *In the Amazon, Pope Francis is setting the agenda for a new kind of synod. America*: The Jesuit Review. https:// www.americamagazine.org/faith/2019/09/12/

8. Allen, Jr., J. L. (2020, Feb. 23). *Pope to US bishops: No, 'synodality' doesn't mean 'democracy.'* Crux. https: //cruxnow.com/news-analysis/2020/02/pope-to-us-bishops-no-synodality-doesnt-mean-democracy/

9. Pope Francis. (2015, Oct. 17). *Ceremony commemorating the 50th anniversary of the institution of the Synod of Bishops: Address of His Holiness Pope Francis.* http: //www.vatican.va/content/francesco/en/speeches/2015/october/documents/papa-francesco_20151017_50-anniversario-sinodo.html

10. Bryson, J. M. (2018). *Strategic planning for public and nonprofit organizations: A guide to strengthening and sustaining organizational achievement* (5th ed.). Wiley.

11. Collins, J. C., & Porras, J. I. (1996, Sept.). Building your company's vision. In *On Strategy* (pp. 77–102). Harvard Business Review.

12. Berger, W. (2012, Sept. 17). *The secret phrase top innovators use.* Harvard Business Review. https: //hbr.org/2012/09/the-secret-phrase-top-innovato

Printed in Great Britain
by Amazon

54650411R00076